D0187459

Just Listen More Intense

Korrie Morrow

Detroit Ink Publishing

Detroit, Michigan USA

Copyright

Just Listen More Intense

By Korrie Morrow

ISBN: 978-0-9970126-2-0

Cover Design by Sydnee Turner, SydGrafix Design Specialist

http://sydgrafix.com

Published by Detroit Ink Publishing

http://detroitinkpublishing.com

4444 2nd Avenue

Detroit MI 48226 USA

Dedication

I dedicate this book to my son, Korrie Morrow Jr.

Son, you are the motivation behind everything I do.

I love you with all of my heart.

I also dedicate this book to all of my social media followers.

Thank you for keeping me inspired. I truly appreciate all of your support.

Acknowledgements

To my mother, Dr. Shanda Evans:

Thank you for imparting your wisdom and spiritual guidance in the chapters that include your notes. Your support means the world to me.

To my aunt, Claudette Pendleton:

Thank you for offering your editing expertise. I couldn't have done this without you.

To my good friend, Michelle Rogers:

Thank you for your sweet encouragement and wisdom. I'll see you at the top!

Introduction

This is my second book. A more Intensified Explanation of why the relationship is or isn't succeeding. I will not be giving you practical tools to succeed but I will be going to the very core of your heart and dealing with your secret thoughts, what you plan to do, and have been doing. This is your personal guide that will provide the information you need to prepare for the new season of your life. The stories in this book are all inspired by true events. Warning- I will be going deep! So, buckle up, and get ready for a real ride. Just Listen.

Table of Contents

LETTING GO OF NEGATIVITY

1. Never Settle

Stop entertaining a counterfeit relationship. It makes zero sense for your future. So many people are in relationships that are being forced. They are in relationships that are missing key components: unconditional love, trust, loyalty, patience, and compromise. Why settle when you can have the world? Settling is not an option because as time passes, you will regret being with that person and feel like you wasted valuable time, so end the game. You should know that you are settling when you have to continuously question your own worth due to the way you are being treated, and you will be scared to talk about the issues with him or her. You should always feel safe to talk to your loved one about your feelings! Understand? If you have to remind your partner every week that you need attention and affection, you are settling. How can someone go a year without touching his or her spouse? You must wake up, smell the coffee, and move on. You need the love to be mutual; it's much easier to love when two people are on the same page. There should be no settling just because you guys have kids or share household responsibilities. Create your own lane, and let God lead your way. Don't worry about how much time you've spent on someone. It's not about where you have been; it's about where you are going. Yes, this is true! It takes faith, so stop holding on to a situation that's not good for you and not flourishing. Every relationship has its problems, so I'm not talking about just throwing people away just for the heck of it. I'm talking about settling in a relationship that is destructive to you either physically, emotionally, mentally, or in any way that's destructive to you and, therefore, obviously, not good for you.

2. Letting go of Negative People

In order to thrive- whether it be financial growth, spiritual growth, or emotional growth- you have to let go of negative environments and the negative people in your life. Negative people are the greatest destroyers of self-confidence and self-esteem. I know that sometimes it's hard to let go of people you hold dearly, but if they are negative and always pessimistic, they need to go.

Let me tell you about Jasmine. Jasmine was raised by her single mother. Her father left when she was a baby and never reached out to her, so she grew up with a broken heart. She watched her mother drift in and out of volatile relationships. She was never shown a standard of how men should treat women. As an adult, Jasmine allowed men to disrespect her- believing that this type of treatment was okay. She didn't know how to respond or to care enough for herself to walk away from that type of treatment. She just didn't know that she deserved better. She would turn to her friends for advice, and they would tell her things like, "Just do him like he does you," or, " Girl, he's fine! So what if he doesn't want you to go to school." Say what?

Notes from Dr. Shanda R. Evans

Life and death is in the power of the tongue!! A Python is a symbolic form of a strength killer. A Python will slowly drain you of all your power, strength and fluids in your body. It wraps its body around your body until you are nothing. This is what a negative atmosphere or environment or even a person will do. Become energetic and creative. Surround yourself with vision seekers, and watch growth occur!

Ladies, be careful from whom you take advice. If someone gives you this type of advice, they are not your friends. They just want you to be like them: sad, depressed, and nasty. It's time to listen to your instincts. Your mom probably told you years ago who were and were not your genuine friends, and you know momma always knows best. Real friends will lead you to God and tell you what is right. You know who the poisonous snakes are in your circle, so it's time to rid yourself of the venom. You need to allow yourself space to grow. If you're not losing friends, you're not growing. Change is always a good thing. Healthy relationships with friends and family should not cause you pain or hinder your progress. They should only uplift you, so take a stand, and look up to God. Don't be scared to leap out on faith and learn how to fly!

3. Never be a Number

If someone is seeing more than one person, texting more than one person, or messaging more than one person, leave them alone. You deserve to be the only one; you deserve way more. Girl, it's true! Toughen up. You grown, right? Stop thinking that you can change a person because you can't. Just because someone says something doesn't mean that it's true. People will use kids to be around their kids' mother. They will stay married while giving you broken promises. You'll always be number two. If a man is married or with his child's mother when he meets you, he will never leave them for you. Never accept being an option. Hitting home yet?

This reminds me of a beautiful young woman named Asia. She was very kind hearted- the type of woman who would put others needs before her own needs, but at the age of 23, she was divorced with two daughters. Heartbroken and lonely, she began seeking comfort, and she found it in a young man named Trey. Trey was two years younger than her, nice looking, charismatic, and soft- spoken, but he was a street guy. They quickly became close friends, and spent several months talking on the phone and texting one another. They talked about everything, and Asia began to trust him. She started confiding in him and sharing her sacred feelings and the most intimate details about her life. They started to grow feelings and took their friendship to the next level. After they slept together, Trey did a 360 and completely changed. Knowing how vulnerable she was, he began manipulating her to the point where she had fallen so hard for him that she could not let go. Soon, Trey started

16

living with another woman. Although Asia knew about the other woman, she continued to allow Trey to come and go as he pleased because she could not let go. Asia knew she was merely an option to Trey and not a choice, but she was so emotionally invested that it hurt too much to not have him in her life at all, so she accepted him part-time.

The problem is you have to be careful with who you open up to because the devil always comes in disguise, appearing as an angel of light, but after he's deceived and deluded you, his true colors are revealed. Men will come into your life, make you feel like you can trust them, and then use your vulnerability to control you. Sometimes, this is not even their intent, but once they see that you have opened up to them, they realize the power they have over you. You should never be ok with being a number! If your heart is unsettled, the first step is to pray. Ask God to order your footsteps, and to give you the heart and mind to be okay with his answer and leading. Asia prayed to God that if Trey was her assigned mate, God would give her the tenacity to wait for him to stop being a fool. Trey wasn't her assigned mate. Two weeks later, Trey was shot dead in the streets.

4. Wanting Someone Who Doesn't Want You

If you entertain a fictitious relationship, you risk missing your designated king or queen. Someone who cannot see your innate value does not deserve to occupy space in your precious heart. Just listen.

Take Janee, for instance, a very kind and loving woman in her early thirties and emotionally attached to Pete, a hard-working man and the love of her life. They had been dating for 15 years, but Pete had been married for 20 years. Pete had been promising Janee that he would leave his wife for years, but would always use his kids as an excuse. Janee would feel sorry for Pete every time he would bring up his kids, so she settles for being number two. She must build her strength by praying and asking the Lord to break the ungodly soul tie between her and Pete. Janee must be willing to let go in order to be truly happy with someone who sees only her. She wants him, but she doesn't realize that he doesn't want her. He wants to be with his wife. Ladies, if he is not doing *everything* possible to show you that he wants you and *only* you, then please *stop* wasting your time. It's time to love yourself a little more than that!

When you want someone who doesn't want you, you are blocking your God chosen mate's view of you.

Notes from Dr. Shanda R. Evans

Loneliness is what it all boils down to. To keep yourself from being lonely and needing someone to care for you, you settle! Make a vow to yourself that you will stop yourself from being used and abused. Hurt if you have to, but fill yourself with daily activities such as work, going out with friends and family, attending church, and giving more time to self-development.

---

5. Pay Attention to These Signs

If a person can go a whole day without talking to you, then tell him or her to go a couple of more! If they don't care enough to check up on you and see how your day is going, then take that as a sign. If they go five or six hours without returning your text, then don't explain what took them so long. It's a sign. If you tell them about something important like a potential promotion or a doctor's appointment, and they don't call or text to see how it went- sign. If you are always the one to initiate contact- sign. If you tell them about something they did that upset you, but they are not apologetic and instead have excuses- sign. If they are only attentive when they need something from you- sign. If they take from you but rarely give- sign. If you do things for them and they seem unappreciative- sign. If you feel like you are being used- sign. Need I say more? These are all signs that they are not genuinely interested in you. Pay attention and don't ignore the signs. Are you listening? The warning signs are always there, but you can't be blinded by the sun.

Some people will go weeks, months, and even years without reaching out to you and then try to come back into your life expecting you to care for their feelings. Don't do it! And when their regular calls and texts become far and few in between, that's when you know it's time to keep it moving. Turn that page. Next chapter!

6. Never Chase Someone

Train yourself to stop entertaining old texts messages, old pictures, and old memories. Keyword: OLD! If you continuously look at these things, you will get in your feelings. Stop yourself and find productive things to do that make you happy. Ease your mind and spirit.

Ebony, 18, was a sweet girl. She had no experience with love and fell straight in love with a much older and experienced guy named Kobe 28. When they met, he had a girlfriend, but Ebony, being young and growing up without a father, didn't understand the concept of self-respect, so she continued sleeping with Kobe while he continued to be with his girlfriend and several other women. Eventually he began abusing Ebony, hitting her, disrespecting her, calling her ugly and nasty, telling her no man will ever want her. But still she would go back and stay by his side, thinking she would never find anyone better because he had belittled her so much that she forgot who she was. This behavior, she learned as a child. Her mother accepted mistreatment from men, so she did too. She became obsessive of Kobe and would follow him wherever he'd go. She would search through his car, his phone, and his pockets. She often found condoms, panties, and women's clothing, yet she would still stay.

One day she went to the doctor because she wasn't feeling well. It turns out she was pregnant. When she told Kobe, he disappeared and just left her out in the cold to recover. He was not there for her in her time of need. She never went back to his sorry behind again and ended up having and raising this child on her own. She spent years chasing after Kobe, and in the end he left her when she needed him the most.

If you are feeling quite lonely and in despair, find something to do that will take your mind off of the person. Pray, work out, read some books. Read my books!

7. Loving From a Distance

Sometimes you are better off loving people from a distance. There are some people in your life who will drain you of all your mental energy. You have to start loving yourself more and focus on your personal goals, your children, and your right to be treated as a king or queen.

There was a man named Mo. Mo was a very humble and kind, God-fearing man. He was well established in his career and ready to share all that he had with the right woman. He thought he found that right woman in Denise. When he met Denise, she was emotionally torn apart and broken, but he was mesmerized by her beauty and her body and instantly fell in love with her. He gave all that he had to offer to Denise and loved her in a way that every woman dreams about. Soon, they were expecting their first child, but Denise became bored with Mo. She enjoyed the thrill of a bad boy and wasn't ready for the type of man that Mo was. Six months after she had their child, she abruptly left Mo and moved out. Mo became depressed and lost all faith, feeling like he could not live without her. Three years passed, and Denise came back and eased her way back into Mo's life. Mo let her back in because he was still in love with her, and so they gave it another shot. They had three more children together, but things started to go downhill because Mo had gotten laid off and was struggling to find another job. They were struggling financially which was causing a lot of stress for the both of them. Once again, Denise left Mo; this time for a man who currently had more to offer. After a couple of years passed, again she tried to come back, but Mo was tired. He decided that he was not going to give the relationship another chance. Although he still loved her, he knew his love for her was better placed from afar.

It's OK to keep distance between yourself and someone you love. If you continue to let people who hurt you remain close, you will find yourself in constant disappointment growing bitter and angry. And

I know you don't have time for that. You're too busy leveling up! Right? I'll wait.

8. Never Let Someone Disrespect You

At the first sign of disrespect, leave! Why are you putting up with disrespect? Do you enjoy being called out of your name, lied to, or cheated on? Wake up! Respect Yourself!

There was this guy, Jonah. He was 28 years old, playboy type. He loved using women. He could get anything he wanted out of them: money, cars, housing. He met a nice 26 years old woman online. Sheila had never been with a man before and she was intrigued by Jonah's knowledge and handsome looks. They began talking on the phone and texting everyday. Sheila lived in California and Jonah lived in Indiana, so they kept communication through phone calls, texting, and skyping. As their relationship progressed, Jonah started to speak to Sheila disrespectfully, often saying things like, "Shut up when I'm talking to you," and "Do what I say or you won't hear from me again."

Because Sheila was inexperienced in relationships and uncomfortable with confrontation and standing up for herself, she would continuously allow these types of exchanges, not realizing she was opening the door for greater disrespect in the future. Just the sound of his voice could make her melt, and she would forgive him every time. She eventually grew to love him. Jonah started to take trips out to California to see Sheila every few months. She would always pay for his flight and began sending him money on a regular basis. This went on for a few years, and Sheila believed that she was in a long distance relationship with the man of her dreams.

One year for Valentine's Day, she decided to surprise him, so she told him that she might come visit him one day soon. This made Jonah angry and he told her she can't come because he was too busy with work - sign. She had his address from sending money Western Union to him, so she flew to Indiana and showed up at his doorstep unannounced. She was shocked and heartbroken to see that he lived in a beautiful home with his wife and children. When he came to the door he acted like he didn't know her and made it seem like she was just some crazy lady.

You see, people who disrespect you are disrespectful because they are full of themselves, prideful, selfish, and arrogant, and maybe even narcissistic. They have no regard for how their actions affect other people. Sheila wanted to scream and yell and hit him, but she knew there was no use. So, she politely apologized for the confusion and walked away. She never contacted Jonah again, and she never allowed another man to show her any sign of disrespect.

9. Every Situation Does Not Call for a Reaction

Never let someone see you sweat or behave out of your normal character. When people see they are pushing you to a point where you are losing your self-control, they feel triumphant. Maybe it's a DM you received from your boyfriend's ex- girlfriend or a screenshot of some inappropriate texts that your spouse sent. Whatever the circumstance is, don't react impulsively. Instead, remain calm and wait for God to work. He will provide clarity for you, so you can make good decisions.

When someone is cheating on you, lying to you, and talking down to you, it's time to make a change. You have to be able to move on without an explanation! They know what they did, and you don't have to explain why you are leaving. When a person is bringing you down and changing who you are and the way you see yourself, it's time keep it moving. Take note of the lessons learned from this relationship and end that chapter of your life, so you can prepare yourself for the next chapter. Breathe and keep on living.

10. Open Your Eyes Before it's too Late

Open your eyes. You can lose your life by being with someone who is violent. You can catch a deadly disease by being with someone who is unfaithful. You can put yourself and your kids in danger by being with someone who is an alcoholic or a drug addict. This will not only affect you but everyone around you! Sometimes deep love can blur your vision. The heart and the brain are not always on the same page, but usually, your brain is right. Trust your instincts.

In this world, when you are doing well, and people see you growing, the devil will send distractions to disrupt your growth, and sometimes you don't realize it until it's too late. This is why it's so vitally important to remain watchful and prayerful as God's book tells us to. You must stay focused and keep your eyes on the prize. Trust the Lord, and he will protect you. We've all been in situations where we have turned a blind eye to someone who was taking advantage of us or deceiving us. Well, your eyes are wide open now. You can see straight through the games and the manipulation. Drop that heavy load. You are better off without the old and will be even better with the new. The new you.

11. Flipping the Script

Have you ever felt alone in a relationship? Like the feelings are very one sided, and every time you bring it to your loved one's attention, he or she flips things back on you? And, you accept it because you feel you love the person. That is not love; it's an ungodly soul tie that needs to be broken.

A girl by the name of Rachel was just turning 21. She was a loyal girl and hadn't had many boyfriends, so she was naive about the games that guys play. She caught the attention of Milo, a handsome guy that all the girls wanted. He approached her, sweet talked her, and before you knew it, she was head over heels in love. Rachel was a naturally giving person, so when it came to Milo, she didn't hold back. She bought him clothes, shoes, and gave him money all the time. Milo would please her sexually, in exchange, to blind her to the fact that he wasn't doing half of what she was putting out. He was taking advantage of her. She was proud to be the girlfriend of a guy she knew so many other women wanted.

One day while scrolling through Instagram, Rachel saw a picture of Milo out with a pretty girl, and the caption read, *Fun times with a friend from high school*. She later found inappropriate pictures of the same girl in Milo's phone. Come to find out, this girl was an ex-girlfriend and not just a friend. When she confronted Milo, he of course lied straight to her face. Rachel was strong. She broke up with him and never looked back. Leave at the first sign of disrespect and never let someone waste your time twice.

12. Trust More When the Time is Right

You have to stop putting your *full* trust into a man and woman. They will fail you. The Bible teaches us to trust the Lord with *all* of our hearts, not people. Even when it's a good man or woman, you are still not to place your full trust in anyone, but God! (Proverbs 3:5-6). Men and women will tell you whatever sounds right to get what they want, so you must use the knowledge that your parents taught you when you were growing up. Remember now, momma ain't raise no fool! You're a strong woman of God. And to the fellas, your father ain't raise no push over. King up! Take yourself and your dignity back. Most of all, you must pray to God to lead your decision- making. Scriptures tell us to acknowledge God in all of our ways, and He will direct our paths. In time, your special, right person will show you that they are trustworthy, but know that it is a mistake to trust too soon because that is how we all end up getting hurt. Take time to really get to know the person before making up your mind to give him or her your heart. Think about it. Why does it hurt so badly when someone we care about betrays us or lies to us? It's because we trusted them. That is just the sad reality. So protect your heart and enter relationships with caution. God will tell you when it's ok to trust and let your guard down. Until then, stop trying to do it your way and let go. God's got this.

13. Temptation

Stay strong my brother and sister. It's not that serious especially if you end up ruining a marriage or disrespecting yourself. Giving yourself to someone that doesn't commit to *only you* is like selling yourself short. It's punishing yourself. Sometimes experience is the teacher.

Once there was a man named Paul. He was 17 years young and eye candy to the ladies. He was growing into manhood and noticed that all the ladies found him attractive and that started to pump his head up. He was young and wanted to experience life, so he ignored the lessons that his mother and father taught him- that sleeping with more than one woman can only lead to problems. Paul had a girlfriend and a child that he loved, but he kept cheating on her and giving her STD's over and over again. He took it as a joke! He knew that he was wrong, but he just could not resist the temptation of so many pretty women seeking his attention. It wasn't clicking in his head that his girlfriend would leave him and take his son with her until one day he came home to learn that his girlfriend had left with his son and went to another state. He was shocked and devastated, but she had had enough. For her, the game was over.

Sometimes a person has to leave in order for one to learn. Paul repeatedly gave into temptation and did not value the gem that he already had in his girlfriend. Sometimes your struggles will make you the strong person you are today! Paul began to learn how to fight temptation by going back to his biblical roots that he was taught as a child. He surrendered, and God opened his eyes to see that it was just an ungodly sexual and mental tie that needed to be broken. Till this day he still regrets losing his son's mother because he has not met another woman who compares to her. The lesson here is simple. When you give into temptation, you risk losing the people who matter most.

14. Never Pay for Attention

Don't ever try to make a person love you. Love is natural. Love just happens. There is nothing you can do to make someone love you. The best relationships happen unexpectedly. So if someone thinks that he or she is better than you, kindly, but boldly tell the person that he or she would be better off by him or herself. A lot of the times, when you let go, people will come back trying to make you feel bad by luring you back in with fake kindness. Don't believe it! Words mean nothing. Actions are key! Tell that person that you're from the "show me" state.

Lexy was one of those women who would pay for everything to buy her man's love and attention. She paid for dinners, trips, and helped him maintain his lifestyle, and he still entertained other women by taking them on dates and texting them. Hitting home? I know this sounds familiar. Trying to buy a man's attention will not work. It *will not* make him love you. It'll just make him use you even more. Don't be mad. You perpetuated his behavior. All the money and gifts in the world won't make him love you. If he is depleting your account instead of helping you build your account, drop him!

15. Don't Disrespect Yourself

Rule number one: take care of yourself first. No one can take better care of you than you! Exercise your mind, your body, and your soul, and stay focused on your goals. Negative energy will attack you daily to try to get you off balanced. That's why you need God to protect you. You will fail if you try to fight alone. You have to fight spirit with spirit. When you surround yourself with people who do not have your best interest at heart, you are disrespecting yourself. When you don't take time to nourish your brain and your body, you are disrespecting yourself. When you give up and accept defeat, you are disrespecting yourself. How can you demand respect from other people if you haven't demanded respect from yourself?

16. Venting is Good

Stop venting to everyone and telling them your deepest life problems. It's human nature for people to get a little enjoyment from hearing about people who are in worse situations than themselves. You must only open up to someone you can trust, someone who you know loves and understands you. People with sour intentions will use what you tell them against you. Venting is good. It's healthy but only to the right person. When you don't have anybody to vent to, remember that God always hears your cry. God loves you. And, the beautiful thing about talking to God is that you never have to question his motives. Counselors are also good to vent to; it's their job. Avoid talking to just anybody who's willing to hear you out because your weak moments make you an easy target of manipulation. Even if there are not current solutions to your problems, talking about them always helps you feel better. Talking about them will bring you clarity, so do talk and vent out your frustrations, but just be mindful about who you choose to be the listener. Please be careful of who you choose to trust.

17. Don't Let Idiots Train Your Day

Negative attacks will happen daily, but never allow people to come in and ruin your happiness. You have to master the art of curving people when necessary. When focusing on a task, you must block out others in order to successfully complete that task. If you entertain the problems of others, it will distract you from what you have to do, and you will perform poorly. So you must prioritize and put things in order to take care of your business first because you can't help others without helping yourself first.

18. Controlling Jealousy

Jealousy- it's a universal emotion among human beings. It comes without warning. You see or hear something and all of a sudden you're pierced with feelings of envy, anger, fear, sadness, and humiliation. You are now consumed with negative thoughts, and the natural state of your spirit is tainted with uneasiness and discomfort. We have all been there before. It's a terrible feeling, but once it comes, it's here. You wish you could send it back, but you can't. There is nothing you can do about it. We cannot control whether or not we get jealous;

we can only control how we act on jealousy's behalf. We can also pray to God about delivering us from jealousy if it's a constant problem. It's also important to meditate on pure thoughts and to develop a thankful attitude to curb feelings of jealousy. If you're a grateful person, it's not so easy to have constant feelings of jealousy.

Jealousy has been the downfall of many relationships, friendships, and familial bonds. It causes people to behave irrationally and make impulsive decisions. This is why having trust in a relationship is so important. There will always be other men or women who are attracted to your partner. There will always be attacks on a seemingly happy relationship, but you have to trust that your loved one values you enough to not breathe truth into your jealousy. If there is something that is making you jealous, don't make assumptions or allow faulty scenarios to overtake your mind. Instead, talk to your spouse and allow him or her to assuage your insecurities. There is only one 'you' on this earth, and 'you' are special. You are the person that your mate fell in love with. Take pride in knowing that you are irreplaceable. The last thing a faithful person wants to deal with is a jealous partner who is always making accusations, so when you feel jealousy approaching, assess whether the emotion is really warranted, but be careful with how you react to those emotions. If you are with someone who has jealous tendencies, do your best to make them feel secure in your loyalty, but if the jealousy is too surreal, you may need to run for your life. The effects of jealousy can damage a relationship, but only when the person with an unwarranted jealousy problem lets it drive them. "For where jealousy and selfish ambition exist, there will be disorder and every vile practice" (James 3:16).

19. Recognize Game

Talk is cheap. Just because they said it doesn't mean they meant it. People are charming. They will tell you lies and fill your head with hope. Don't be a sucker for words. Listen to their actions. One of the most manipulative moves is crying to seem sorry, but that's exactly what they are- sorry! So let them cry like a child, and stop giving chances to people who don't deserve another chance. Keep reading while they keep pleading. You're getting stronger. I can tell!

20. Marriage is Sacred to God and 3 is a Crowd

Listen closely. There's a twist to this one. There are negative and positive family interferences, and you must be able to tell the difference between the two. First is the positive. When a true friend, mother, father, or close relative can tell something isn't right or that you're in danger of hurting your future, and they show concern, you must let them help you. If you're offended by positive interferences, you'll push their love away, and you could be missing an important wake up call. No one enjoys their family interfering in their relationship, but if you miss the message they are trying to get to you, you will have to face problems all alone, which sometimes can lead to making even more wrong choices that can hinder you for a lifetime.

Then you have negative interferences. This is when family will try their hardest to break up a happy home because they fear losing a loved one to someone else. Ever had your boyfriend or husband's mother try to tell you what to do and how to treat her son? Or try to run your house when she didn't even live there? Hit home yet? If you and your partner are happy, you must be mature enough to stand up to your parents and tell them that you love and respect them but you're grown now and need some space and respect in your relationship. Yes, sometimes parents, relatives, or friends can ruin your relationships if you let them, so don't.

HEALING TAKES TIME

21. Stay Strong and Keep it Moving

Life will prevail. It gets better in time. Time heals all scars. At first it might be hard because you have a big and soft heart towards him or her. God is the only answer to your problems. Think about it. You've tried just about everything possible to excel in life, and be happy, but yet you seem to go backwards or you spend time thinking about someone who really wouldn't care if you lived or died. You must pray to God to heal your mind and lead your steps. It's not your battle; it's the Lord's. You need unbelievable faith in order to move forward. Think of it like this, when Michael Jordan had 10 seconds on the clock, and the team gave him the ball, it took faith that he would hit the shot to win the game, but he'll never know unless he tries! A relationship is the same way. If you think you can't live without a person, you won't move forward, but if you trust that you can, you will. It's a mind -set. We are fearfully and wonderfully created. God has given us the ability to accomplish what we put our minds to.

In order to move forward with your life, you have to forgive him or her, but never forget what they did and how they mistreated you. Remembering how they treated you will help you to not go back to a dead situation, and forgiving the person will help you to let him or her go and move on with your life to better things.

22. A Made Up Mind

Pull back from seeing the significant other. Stay positive and keep moving forward. Drop all of the "negative" people around you that keep pulling you backwards.

Listen to Jackson's story. He was a college athlete, handsome, intelligent, and very arrogant. He met Babygirl- tall, nice figure, brown eyes, quiet, and smart- when she was still in high school. After a couple of dates, she fell in love with him. Sleeping with him made her feel like she was in love when it was really just an unholy sexual tie. Jackson was very smooth with his words; he knew exactly what to say to make her melt. Although he didn't deserve it, she began giving him everything he wanted: money, sex, meals, and encouragement. He knew that he could disrespect her, cheat on her, and take advantage of her, and she would never leave him. Once in awhile she would build up the courage to leave, but as soon as he started apologizing, professing his love, and swearing that he had changed, she would run right back to him.

Never let a boy make you think it's OK to act like you're his mother and take care of him. There is nothing wrong with helping your man in his time of need, but you want a man who can hold his own and lead you. You are his strength, but he is your leader. If a guy puts himself in a position of being your son instead of your man, drop him. You must leave for good in order for him to learn from his mistakes.

One day after a heated argument, Jackson kicked Babygirl out of his house. She became so overcome with sadness that it made her physically ill. Sometimes a person has to get hurt to the point of being physically sick before they realize the changes they need to make. Jackson tried to call her and run his same "come back baby" game, but Babygirl was done. He expected his game to work like always, but like R.Kelly said, "When a woman's fed up, there ain't nothing you could do about it." She had to leave him in the past in order to grow. If not, she would've stayed in the same mental tie that needed to be broken.

People will use you over and over again until you stop letting them! You control your life. This abuse will only continue for as long as *you* allow it. So, declare it "No more!" They don't want you; they just want what you can do for them. Stop being goofy and getting played. When someone is using you, it's like you're a prisoner, but you have the power to set yourself free. What are you going to do? Remain a prisoner or be free? This is your life. Choose wisely!

23. Steps of Moving Forward

Thoughts of the person will not leave your mind quickly. So, God wants you to ponder on doing what you need to do to prevent making the same mistake twice because if you entertain it, you will start falling backwards, and back into the game of being played you go. You must let go!

There was this woman named Kim. She was 23 - beautiful hourglass figure, great cook, and an overall amazing woman. When she met Leo, 25, handsome, and nicely built, she knew he was the one for her. Their relationship was seemingly perfect and they were planning to get married soon. But one day Leo had an unexpected death in his family. It was someone who was very close to him. This loss consumed his mind. He started neglecting his relationship and Kim's needs. He began drinking heavily to null the pain, which made the situation even worse. His drinking caused him to be angry all the time, and he took his anger out on Kim, but she loved Leo, so she tried her best to be patient and understanding with him. This went on for about a year, and Kim tried to stick it out. She couldn't forget the person he used to be-the perfect man. She prayed and prayed, and eventually made the decision to leave. This left Leo alone and depressed. He often found himself feeling sorry for himself and drunk while texting her. Kim would fall victim, respond and end up disappointed again.

The first step in moving forward would be to ignore the text messages and the "I love you" phone calls. But since Kim didn't, Leo would lure her into sleeping with him which made her feel a love connection, but it was only a sexual tie. Secondly, you need to get closer to God by reading the word of God for spiritual protection and strength to fight temptation. But now that Leo could see Kim was loving him again, he began to tell her she would never find another man that wants her because she's ugly and stupid. Don't allow anyone to make you doubt your worth. It's going to be hard. You will think you're never going to find anyone else, but you will triumph through this. You have to go through the pain before you have the strength to see the sunshine. You must have unbelievable faith. Well, Kim finally left for good, and he was sorry to see her go. In spite of how he treated her, he really did love her. Lost and hopeless, he had no choice but to turn to the Lord. Now, Leo is a changed man. Gotta thank God for the comeback. Once a man loses something completely, sometimes it helps him to never take his blessings for granted ever again. He'll learn to appreciate what he has.

24. Keep Hope Alive

I know that you are hurt, but let me give you a pointer that will help you not to be a fool again. I know you've heard it a million times, but just listen. OK? Talk yourself happy. There is power in the tongue. I remember when I lost everything, and I went to church with my mother. As I listened to the pastor, he was saying a prayer and asked the church to repeat it. I did and accepted it. The next day I received a new three- bedroom house and blessings just started to overflow. Just think about the time in your life when things weren't happening like you wanted, but when you asked God to help, he delivered right on time! Can somebody say Amen? God is faithful. Recognize that and be thankful. Yes, lay it over to him and trust the process.

25. Never too Late to Start Over

My mother always said, "Your latter will be greater than your former." There was a woman, Becky, who had gotten pregnant at a very young age, and she was from a strict family that would not tolerate her living in their home with a child out of wedlock. So, at 18 years old, she married Lucky who was 19. Lucky was a nice, studious, and extremely intelligent young man. His parents believed in him, so they allowed him, his wife, and their newborn daughter to live with them while Lucky finished college. In five years, Lucky had graduated college, secured a decent job position with General Motors and secured a place of their own for himself and Becky. By this time, Becky was a stay home mother and pregnant with their second child. As time went on, Becky began to grow resentful towards Lucky. She knew he was a good man, but she also knew that she was not in love with him when they got married. They hadn't even really known each other that long when she got pregnant, but she felt pressured from both of their parents, so she married him thinking that eventually she would fall in love with him. She faked love and happiness for her family, which is a huge mistake. Lucky, however, did love Becky. He was crazy about her. He loved her so much that he didn't even realize she was not giving him the same quality of love that he was giving her. Five more years passed, and Becky was becoming more and more miserable in her marriage. She found herself treating him meanly and having devilish thoughts. She would daydream about being madly in love with the man of her dreams or being fiercely sexually attracted to the love of her life. She realized that she didn't even know what absolute true love felt like, but she craved it.

After 10 years of marriage, Becky made the gut wrenching decision to end her marriage with Lucky. She was well aware of the depth of sadness this would cause him, their families, and their friends, but she was tired of living a lie. She felt he deserved the chance to be with someone who would obsessively love him like he deserved to be loved. The divorce was messy. Relationships were strained and friends were lost. After the dust settled, Becky found herself a single mother with two kids and lonely. She often cried herself to sleep wondering if she had made a huge mistake. When she found out that Lucky had moved on, she was totally broken. Two years later, Becky had picked up the pieces and was working and doing fine. She started dating a doctor that she met through a friend. Shortly after they started dating, she knew that he was the man of her dreams. In just one year, they were married and the next year they were expecting their first child together.

Becky thought that she had ruined her life by leaving Lucky. But she prayed hard about it, and took a leap of faith and was able to get a second chance at love. She started over, but she is now happier than she's ever been. Don't be afraid to start over if you know you are not living your truth. It's never too late. Love does not have an age limit. Though Becky and Lucky served significant purposes in each other's life, he was not her God chosen mate. She had to endure the pain of hurting and losing loved ones to get to the serene and love-filled place that she is in now. The important thing, however, is to be led by God in your decision to leave a marriage. You must make sure that it's not just a matter of having a rough season in your marriage before you decide to sever a marriage. It's not something you just walk away from without really thinking things through and hearing from God.

26. Having a Good Heart Will Get You Hurt

Of course there are times when you will end up being the one who gives more in a relationship, but make sure that you're really in the right relationship that God wants you in. When you're in the right mutually, caring relationship, it is okay to make sacrifices for one another. But when you know in your heart that you are with a person who is really not good for you and is only using you, never give 100 when you're only receiving 50 back. It doesn't add up and it never will. The person really doesn't care for you. There was a woman named Princess who was an educated and independent woman. She met a street guy named Allen. Allen was a drug dealer and all around hustler. He talked to her for months, mind loving her until she fell in love with his mind. He had done some time in prison, so he was no stranger to talking and faking love for his own comfort. So after a year of sexing him, cooking for him, and letting him make his home in her house, she asked him about their future. He, of course, was very good at evading these difficult conversations. He wasn't interested in committing to her; he just wanted all the perks of a committed relationship. Every time Princess tried to discuss their next steps, Allen would find a way to avoid it. She ignored all of the signs and continued to let him do the same old thing and manipulate the dynamics of their relationship. What you allow will always continue. She started to grow tired of his shenanigans and would tell him she'd had enough and that he needed to leave. But then, he would sweet talk her again and tell her how much he cares about her, how she's the only one for him, and how he just wanted to take things slow, but she started paying attention to the signs. She started wondering why he never took her to meet his parents or why he always went on trips without her. She became suspicious and started snooping and soon found out that he was married with five kids, and two of the five kids were by different women.

Always observe. Take as much time as you need to learn people before you let your heart love hard. He or she has to earn it. Ask yourself what he is doing to deserve all of you. When you have a good heart, you love deeply and you give endlessly, but you are also subjected to experiencing indescribable hurt and pain if you love the wrong person and too quickly. It's sad, but true. Protect your heart. Be cautious about who you allow to experience the magnitude of love you offer. Now, of course, this does not mean that you will never be hurt in some way when you're in the right relationship because no relationship is perfect and no man or woman is perfect. But you surely should not experience disrespect, pain, and dishonor like one does when he or she is in a destructive relationship.

27. A Loss is Sometimes a Gain

Do you feel like you give more than you receive, always paying for something, calling first, texting first, buying birthday gifts and valentine's cards, or telling someone you love them and get nothing in return? There was a man named Matthew. He was from Africa and the relationship morals in Africa are different from America. They believe in fighting for love and never separating once married. He moved to America at age 21 to attend school in America, and this is where he met Summer, an attractive African- American woman. After their first conversation, he knew he was interested in her, but she was a challenging pursuit because she was scarred from being cheated on so many times. Eventually, he earned her trust, and they began dating. After dating for three months, he decided to take her to Africa to meet his parents. His parents loved her. They could tell she was educated and loyal woman.

One evening Matthew went out with his father and accidently left his phone at the house. Bored and nosy, Summer decided to look through his phone. She saw a text from a woman saying she loved and missed Matthew and couldn't wait for him to come home to Africa for a visit. Confused and hurt, she kept quiet until they were headed back to America. When she confronted him, he said that was normal friendship behavior in Africa and the woman was just a friend. So used to getting cheated on, she left him and never went back. She was trying to protect her heart from being hurt again. Matthew tried everything to get her back-called everyday, sent her gifts, wrote her letters- but she never responded.

The stress of her leaving began to make him sick. He was losing weight and losing focus. He didn't understand how someone could leave so easily without talking about it and trying to understand. His mother could see he was at an all time low and began praying with him and speaking life over his body. Matthew began attending church and the word of God began to strengthen him and encouraged him to know that life goes on. He was able to breathe again. Prayer changes things.

Matthew lost the woman he wanted to be with but he gained so much more during the healing process. He emerged a more confident man and more secure in his ability to persevere. He gained recognition of his worth, and most importantly, he established a closer relationship with God. Don't lose yourself while wading through the storm. Instead, trudge through knowing that growth awaits you on the other side. Understand this.

28. Men and Women Fail, but God Never Fails You

Never allow a man or woman to be your God. They will fail you, but God will never forsake you. Through Jesus, all things are possible. There are demons out there that will try to overpower you. You have to be able to recognize the devil's work.

This goes for both men and women. Listen closely. It is not normal for someone to have total control over what you do. You must be able to make your own decisions. It's ok to be submissive to one another, but when someone tries to treat you like they own you, telling you where you can and cannot go or what you can and cannot do, they are controlling you. They are trying to be your God, but they can't, so don't let them. Stop holding back and take control of your life. Be the virtuous king or a queen of your own life. Respect one another's freedom. Don't try to take anyone's voice away from them. Work together, and pray together.

29. You Can't Force Someone to Change

You have to accept people for who they are and you have to be accepting of who you are. You can do anything to try to change a person or mold them how you want them to be, but it will never work. They might try to change and improve for a while, but deep inside that person is still who and how God made them to be. So, the best way is to love and accept who they are, and to find the right someone who loves and accepts who you are. People are who they are. Think about it. Some of you have been with people for 5, 10, or even 30 years and they have never changed in the ways you want them to change. Granted, as people grow, they will have some natural changes that occur within themselves, but these changes are leading them to become the person they are supposed to be. It is what it is. If you can't accept her or him as they are, then leave. You both deserve better. It takes two to make it work, so that means both have to put forth effort.

Please do not get go into relationships knowing there are things you want to change about your partner and thinking you will be able to make them change. This is a recipe for disaster. If someone wants to change, he or she will take the necessary steps to do so, but change is not something that can be forced.

30. Life Goes On

Listen, you may not see it or feel it, but God has already blessed you with a better life. There is nothing better than letting go of heavy weight from your shoulders. God gives you time to heal and get stronger. So do Mr. King a favor and love yourself more this time. Take care of yourself. Stop letting yourself go by not eating or by eating unhealthily. You don't want to be sick. Eat right, work out, and engage in some retail therapy. Spoil yourself- it's great for the soul. Remember, every storm in your life is temporary. Soon, the sun will shine again, and you will be on your way.

31. Their Loss

Sometimes losing someone is a great thing. Can you imagine having to do everything for an adult? Neediness is exhausting, and when you are always doing things for someone, it can wear you down. But, as soon as you break up, you feel renewed. That's a sign of you letting go of all the negative weight. You feel like you can fly. All those problems are for the next person. You're free. Don't forget to smile. You are rare. Be proud of that. You work hard, cook, dress nice, and have good taste in everything you do. You are the real prize! Yes you! At times, people can be so dumb. They won't realize what they have until it's gone. They weren't ready for the caliber of love that you bring, but that's not your fault. They should have been ready.

32. Sometimes You Have to be Hurt to Wake Up

Sometimes getting hurt is a must because if you never experience pain, you would never know what it feels like to heal and be free. Pain, unfortunately, is a part of the human experience, but it's through the recovery that we truly experience personal growth. If you are hurting and overwhelmed by sadness, just know that it won't last forever. At times, that ache in your heart feels like it's never going to end, but it will, and when it does, you will emerge as a brand new person.

33. Zero Tolerance

Once you let go, keep it that way. Your ex will always try to come back into your life and disrupt your happiness. There was this guy, Carlos that was very soft hearted and always gave people two, three, and four chances before he gave up. He had a girlfriend that he cared about a lot, but the care was not being reciprocated. She would leave him every time they had an argument or when she didn't get her way. A few days later, she would call him apologizing and he would take her back. Their relationship stayed in this pattern for quite a while. But, Carlos began to realize that every time they got back together, he would feel worse instead of better. He noticed that she didn't love him to the capacity that he loved her. So, the next time she left him was the last time. He decided that he wasn't going to take her back even though it hurt. Eventually, he was comfortable with being alone. In order to respect yourself, you must first be OK with being alone. That way you know you can live without someone. Have zero tolerance for people who want to come and go as they please. You are not a revolving door!

34. Toughen Up

It's time for you to toughen up!

1. Feed your mind with positive words. You can do anything you put your mind to. You are a king or a queen, and you deserve to be someone's one and only. You're grown, right? Stop letting people push you around.

2. Recognize who you are. You are a child of God.

3. Discover your purpose. Talk to God and listen for a response. You must submit in order to hear him.

4. Know that God made you for His Glory. You will serve your purpose, for it is already done.

5. Discipline and patience are characteristics and a trademark of God. So, exercise self-discipline and be patient. Your time is coming. So, stay ready, toughen up, and wait for it.

35. Healing Takes Time

You must avoid contact with someone whom you are trying to get over. God has to make you uncomfortable in order for you to not want to go back. When you are lonely, don't call or text that person who hurt you, and don't stalk them on Instagram or Facebook because when they do not text back or when you see a picture of them having fun, you will most definitely digress in your healing process. Instead, do something positive like journaling or enjoying an evening with family or friends.

The healing process is not easy. Your heart is wounded. Your routine has been altered. You feel alone and like no one understands what you are going through. You are mourning the loss of a significant part of your life. Everyday is a challenge. A broken heart is one of life's mysteries. It's something that everyone experiences at some point in his or her life, but it does not last forever. Eventually you will find yourself thinking about him or her less. You will find yourself smiling more and enjoying life again. You *will* feel like yourself again, but you must stay strong through the storm. Do not add difficulty to the process. Hear my voice. Stop entertaining your pain, and you will heal. That person is not God. Believe me, you can survive without him or her. Just listen. This is not a game. No calling. No texting. No stalking. Period.

36. What is Meant to be Will Come to Pass

There is no reason to entertain unauthentic relationships. It will just make things harder. So many people hold on to fake relationships because of the time they've invested! Not on my watch! If someone is not helping you grow or believe in what you do, why are you with them? You don't know? My point exactly! Stop making excuses, and make a change if you want a change! Nothing will happen if you stand still. You must make a move! Take action and make great choices.

Sometimes we fear change. My late father once said to me, "Korrie you will never know unless you try." God is always working; he's just testing your faith. So my message to you is if you're in a relationship that you don't want to be in, change it. Having kids by someone doesn't make that person your life partner. Neither does being high school sweethearts. You can't care or feel sorry for someone else's situation more than you care for your own situation. If so, you will always go back to that someone, and nothing will change. Hitting home? I know it is. Let me stop. Y'all wasn't ready for church! Can I go deeper? If someone is hitting you and being abusive, this is unacceptable! Understand me? Yes you. You must leave now! Run before it's too late. He is not a man. This goes for the ladies also. Yes I said it. A lot of women are abusing their men. So to you men I say don't hit her back, but run! What is meant to be will always come back right. God said it! Maybe love wasn't ready at that time. Sometimes God makes us more mature for one another in the future and sometimes, again, you just need to run!

RECOGNIZE YOUR WORTH

37. Ladies, Recognize Your Worth

One of the worst feelings is discovering that the person you love does not appreciate your value. Ladies, what you need to know is that you have all the power. Your husband will surrender to you, but you must know your worth! Think about it. What are you bringing to the table? Outside of being beautiful and sexy, you work. You cook. You clean. You take care of the home. You manage the bills. You take care of the kids (and sometimes, they're not even your kids). You help them with their homework. You know what day your daughter's recital is on and what time your son's football game starts. Hit home? Not to mention, you are loving. You pray for him. You take your man lunch to his job sometimes. You baked him a cake for his birthday. You always return his texts. You shower and shave before he gets home because you know he's having a rough day at work. You tell him he smells nice and looks good even though he's getting older and may not look like he used to. You bought him a sweater and some jeans while you were out shopping for yourself. You remind him to call his mother on her birthday. You wake up early with the kids so he can sleep in. Queen, you are a superhero. Yes you! And, the truth is, you make men's lives easier. Are you listening?

Now ask yourself, what is he bringing to the table? How does he enhance your life? Is he worthy of you? If the only thing you can say is that you love him, that's not enough. We all know that successful relationships require much more than love. Just because you love someone doesn't mean they are worthy of you and all that you bring. Yes, leaving someone you love hurts beyond measure, but God is here for you. Ask God to give you strength and help you heal. In time, you will be fine, and that's a guarantee! You belong to someone who will recognize your worth, appreciate your value, and thank God for bringing you to them.

38. Fellas, Recognize Your Worth

So much emphasis is always put on what men do wrong and what men aren't doing. But, there are countless great men out there just waiting to meet the right woman- a woman who is worthy of him. Men, it is imperative that you also recognize your worth. Don't allow yourself to be overlooked or disregarded just because there are little boys out here hurting our queens. You have something to offer too. Think about it. What are you bringing to the table? You work long hours at a job that strains your body. After a long day's work, you stop at the store to pick up those few items on the list you were given. You come home and unclog the sink, then you give piggy-back rides around the house. You double-check all the windows and doors before you go to sleep. You tell your woman how pretty she looks when she's wearing sweats with no makeup, and you look at her lovingly when she's undressing to let her know that after three kids, she's still sexy to you.

You make it a point to respond to her texts even though you're busy and don't really feel like texting. You accompany her to baby showers and dinner parties when you would rather be home watching football.

Men, you do a lot. And, it's not your responsibility to have to continuously prove your worth. It is your responsibility to know your worth and her responsibility to appreciate your worth. If you are a king, you need your queen to make your home into a castle. It takes two to make a dream work. Love is a two way street. So ladies if you got a good man and he's been at work all day and comes home tired, make sure you dedicate some time to that man. Fellas, your only relationship goal at this point should be to find the right someone who motivates you to become a better person and show you the potential you didn't see in yourself.

39. Having Respect for One Another

Far too often I meet women who are putting forth effort in their relationships that is not being reciprocated by their men. Never give 100% when the person you are with is really only using you and therefore only giving 50% and oftentimes even less. That is not acceptable! It is not a good feeling when you care more for a person than they care for you. You will begin to put them and their needs before you and your needs.

Take, for instance, this woman I knew named Ashley. Ashley, a teacher, was a natural beauty and very intelligent, but she was very sexual. She had a sex addiction and had to have it. Ashley was in love with Brandon, a hard-working Christian brother who loved God and loved her. Unfortunately, Brandon loved Ashley more than he loved his God because he would do anything to make her smile, even to the point of committing fornication with her, but there was just one problem- he was not a great lover. Ashley would regularly have to pretend to enjoy their intimate time together. Although she loved Brandon dearly, she began to feel more and more unfulfilled with their sex life. She craved a sexual experience that would blow her mind, but she just didn't have the heart to tell Brandon that she was unhappy with his performance.

One day, she ran into an old acquaintance, Marcus, at a party. They didn't know each other well, but had taken a few classes together in college. One drink led to another drink; one thing led to another thing, and they ended up going to a hotel. Marcus pleased Ashley like she had never been pleased before. He gave her multiple orgasms and took her emotions and body to heights that she did not even know existed. Needless to say, she instantly fell in lust with this guy. They continued meeting for five months. She couldn't have been happier. Her relationship with Brandon was going well, and she was getting the sexual pleasure that she desired. Until one day, Marcus disappeared. No replies to her texts, no answers to her calls, no responses to her emails. Nothing. She was confused and devastated. For months, she cried and tried to contact him. She thought that he cared about her, and now, she found herself in a situation where she was with Brandon but always thinking about Marcus. Brandon was giving her his all, but she was not emotionally equipped to do the same.

All of this could have been avoided if she would have just talked to Brandon about the way she was feeling because what they both really needed to do was focus on God more instead of her making sex her god and him making her his. When you are married and in the right relationship, you must have enough respect for your mate to tell them what you would like to see changed in the relationship. You must give each other the chance to improve. It's always best to leave a situation rather than waste someone's time or being deceitful. It's not fair! By the way, shortly after Marcus disappeared, Ashley went to the doctor for a routine check up. It was at this time she learned that she was HIV positive and had most likely gotten Brandon infected as well.

Remember, if you ever have temptation and you desire someone other than your spouse, you need to stay strong. Focus on your kids. Focus on bettering yourself. Focus on making money, and most importantly, focus on getting closer to God. The devil attacks when you're weak, so seek God for protection at all times. Remember that the door swings both ways. You must give respect in order to receive it back. Have enough respect to talk to your spouse in order to work things out before it gets too messy.

40. Keep Your Relationship Low-key

The best advice I can give you is to keep your relationship low-key. Please believe King! People are waiting to break up a happy home. They would love to have what you have. Watch out for haters because haters are real. Haters come in many forms: family, fake friends, co-workers. They are all people who would love to use you just to break your spirit.

A girl called Pinky was a sweet, naive, kind- hearted, free-spirited type of girl. She was just an overall genuine person. When she started dating Kyle, she was overcome with joy. He satisfied her emotional and physical needs. He was the best sexual partner she had ever been with. She would boast about her relationship to family and close friends, not to brag, but because she was authentically fulfilled. Would you believe Kyle ended up sleeping with two of her friends and her mother? Unbelievable- I know! But, it's true! Be careful with whom you confide in. They might be coming through your front door as you're leaving through the back door. And once again, this is why you don't give yourself - your heart and your body to someone so quickly and without them placing a ring on your finger first.

41. Don't Say it if You Don't Mean it

My ex taught me that not every "I love you" is real. People will say they love you just so they can get something out of you or just so you will forgive them. They will make you feel like they love you when they really don't. Love is kind and patient. If someone is telling you they love you too quickly, watch them closely. They may be false. My past relationships have taught me that sometimes people use the word *love* too freely, not knowing what it is to really love someone. It's a powerful word, and when confessed even by the wrong person, those words can make your heart melt and make you forget all the wrong that person has done to you. Many people talk of love with no love action behind it. Actions always speak louder than words. This is especially true for men. Ladies, if you want to know if your man loves you, watch his actions. Men demonstrate their love or lack of love through their actions. Just because someone says it, doesn't mean that it's true. Take your time. Don't rush love. What's the rush? We have a lifetime to go, right? When you rush things, they fall apart quickly. Sometimes, you're too young to really know what love feels like. Get ready. This is about to hit home!

Angie, a young and very beautiful girl, was raised in the suburbs- away from the fast paced hustle of the city. Her parents kept her away from the streets thinking it was the better life. When she left home for college, she was happy to finally be in a big city and on her own. There was a boy, Mikey, in one of her classes who had his eyes on her. He appreciated her beauty and her softness. She was definitely different from the girls he was used to. He was finally able to get her attention and they had an instant connection. Opposites attract! They became best friends and told each other everything about their lives. Their relationship slowly became more and more intimate, so they thought they were meant for one another and started to date. She got pregnant the first time they slept together, so he asked for her hand in marriage saying that he loved her. She knew that she was not sure whether she was completely in love with him, but she thought marriage was the right thing to do. They got married and had their daughter. Angie finished school and started a nice career while Mikey worked hard to support his family.

As they grew older, Mikey fell deeper and deeper in love with Angie. He had completely changed his street ways and was becoming the hard-working and loyal man that women dream of. Only, as Angie got older, she realized that he was not her dream man. She began admitting to herself that she was not in love with him. She suppressed these feelings for 10 years. Although she respected him, believed in him, and loved him as a friend, she knew deep down that she was not romantically in love with her husband. This began to tear her apart. She suffered sleepless nights and days filled with tears because she did not know what to do. She was trapped in a good marriage with a great man that she was not in love with.

What should Angie do? Does she leave a good man and disrupt her family to find her true love? Or does she keep pretending because the grass is never greener on the other side? This is the result of her rushing love and rushing into marriage. If you have to question whether or not you love someone, then you don't love them. She told Mikey she loved him yet she married him knowing that she wasn't sure. Do not tell someone you love them if you don't love them. It is absolutely the cruelest thing you can do to a person. At the end of the day, we all want to be loved, but the pain false love can cause is almost unbearable.

42. Always Put Yourself in Other's Shoes

When thinking of cheating or giving into temptation, always ask yourself, *would I be OK if he or she cheated on me?* The answer is no, right? It doesn't feel good to imagine someone else touching, kissing, and loving your wife or husband.

There was this man named Joe. He was a celebrity and had many female fans or groupies as some may call them, but he also had a girlfriend who loved him to death. Paula, Joe's girlfriend, did any and everything to make him smile. She didn't pay attention to his groupies because she was confident that Joe loved her and knew he respected their relationship enough to never cheat on her. One day Paula received a phone call from Carson, a good friend of Joe's. Carson asked Paula if Joe was around and she said no. He then proceeded to tell Paula that he likes her and that Joe cheats on her all the time. Confused and completely blindsided by this news, she asked Carson if he would meet up with her to discuss this further. They met up and Paula confides in Carson while he comforts her. Soon, they were meeting up for day dates on a regular basis and next thing you know, Paula is pregnant. When Paula's son was born, she knew right away that it was Carson's baby and not Joe's. When the baby was nine months old, she finally confessed to Joe and confronted him about his cheating. Naturally, Joe was outraged knowing that he never cheated on Paula, and when they tried to contact Carson, he was nowhere to be found. Joe broke up with Paula, and despite her multiple attempts to make him stay, he left.

Paula allowed herself to be manipulated and acted out of revenge before even discussing the issue with Joe. Now she's a heartbroken single mother. Always think about how your actions will affect the person you love before you do them. Sometimes people are out to break up your relationship, and will lie just to ruin it. The main point here is always give your spouse the trust you would want if you were in the same situation; it could save your relationship.

43. The Most Difficult Women to Run Game On

Are the Best Ones

Beside every great man is a great woman. Think about it. When you're with the right mate, that woman was made from your rib. She helps you to protect your best thinking ability. So, let her help you grow. Learn from each other. Teamwork. There are two types of women: one will let you do anything you want and will give you husband benefits without marrying her, and the other, it will be difficult to run game on her because she knows her worth. This type of woman is the best because she has standards and demands respect for herself, her body, and her heart. Because she's a strong, virtuous woman, she will see things you may not see and think of things that you may not think of to help you become the best you that you can be. Why? Because she's designed by Almighty God to be your helpmeet. She may see and suggest things to you that you would never think of without her help, and her purpose is to help you step up your game and to reach your highest potential. Now, I'm not talking about a woman who nags and pushes her mate relentlessly. Proverbs 21:9 states that it's better for a man to live on the corner of a rooftop than to share a house with a nagging, quarrelsome wife. A virtuous woman's purpose, although she is a confident woman, is to support her mate and to be his helpmeet, not to nag him and stress him out. So, be thankful for your great woman of virtue if you have one. She respects herself and respects you. She desires success for her life and success for you, too. She's not a self-serving, selfish, or arrogant, vain woman. She is a humble, yet strong, wise, morally, confident woman who not only thinks highly of herself, but of others too. She is a blessing. A good wife is supportive of her husband and encourages you to be better and to grow. If a woman is weak minded, easy to control, having no standards, it will start to rub off on you if you let it! You will become unfocused and her neediness will drain you of your energy. That's why you need the right strong, confident woman who has standards and created just for you. She will add to your foundation. There's nothing like two people on the same page who support one another. Nothing can stop their success.

44. A Real Man Sees Only You

Even at your worst times, the people who love you unconditionally will never leave. John and Jenny were high school sweethearts. They were living the American Dream: beautiful kids, nice home, and flourishing careers. For years they were happy and traveled the world with their kids having amazing adventures! Jenny became sick, and at a routine checkup, her doctor told that he spotted cancer in her throat. Jenny could not believe what she was hearing. She prided herself on being healthy and taking great care of her body. She became stressed and anxious thinking about how John would feel. Would he look at her differently? So she hid it from him for a couple of months until her declining health became noticeable. She finally told him about it, and he cried for hours and then said to her, "Let's pray baby. God's got us. He will see us through this." Everyday thereafter, John prayed for his wife and his family. Seeing her strength through all that she was going through made John love his wife even more.

Pay close attention ladies because it's in these types of situations when those who claim they love you will show you their true colors. If he leaves you when things hit the fan, he is not for you. This messages goes to the fellas as well. If she leaves when things get hard, don't let it bother you. She is doing you a favor. Back to the story, so Jenny was scheduled to have surgery in two days to remove the cancer. John took a leave of absence from work for the rest of the year to be by his wife's side (real man). She recovered 100% and life went on beautifully. She was scared that John would see her differently or lose attraction towards her due to her illness, but if a man truly loves you, he will always only see you- your heart, your soul, and your spirit. A real man recognizes that a woman is more than her outward appearance. If he does not stand by your side during your critical time of need, why are you holding on?

45. Every Person Does Not Love the Same

Pay attention to the signs. Again, if you are the one who is calling, texting, and taking him or her out all the time, take a minute to review your partner's love language so you can understand how they show love and how they appreciate being shown love.

There was a pastor named Drew. Pastor Drew had an abundance of wisdom in the word and was faithful to the Lord. His wife, however, although she was his co-pastor, was not as committed to the word as he was, but she loved her husband and children tremendously. After three kids and 10 years of marriage, she began to feel lonely. Pastor Drew was always working. She began feeling temptation for other men because she didn't have the protection of the Lord due to half stepping in her love and service to the Lord. She didn't understand her husband was a chosen man of God that couldn't give all his attention to her. It's a sacrifice that some of us pay to balance God's will. Pastor Drew showed most of his love through loving God, being a faithful husband, and taking care of home. He didn't quite understand that his wife needed to be shown love through more quality time and intimacy. Without a doubt God comes first before all, but you must not forget to make time for your wife, and raising your kids. He gave them to you. We are still human and have feelings. And to the wives and husbands alike, it is vital that you recognize and determine who's the mate for a lifetime and who's not. A lot of people are leaving marriages for only temporary happiness.

46. A Loyal Man is a Great Man

It's time to break the cycle from generation to generation. Cheating and having many women is not cool, sexy, or being a man. It's nasty, and it's degrading to men and women. Once you get older, you realize that being with several women is overrated. You risk catching diseases and bearing children that you're not prepared to love and raise properly. However, if you listen, you will learn something and avoid learning the hard way. My grandmother used to say, "A hard head makes a soft behind," yet people still choose to learn the hard way which could lead to stress, child support, hatred, unforgivingness, sickness, and even death. When you live like this, you block God's blessings. But when you submit, the gates open for God to deliver blessings to you. So stop following young minded curses and make a new way. Be a leader, not a follower. If you trust in God, He will see your way through.

47. Get What You Deserve

You deserve some peace after all that you have been through. You deserve to be happy. You deserve to be loved unconditionally. Why settle when you can have it all? If you had two job offers - one as a cook at McDonald's and the other as a manager of a nursing home- which one would you choose? Exactly. See how easily you made that decision. Do the same when it comes to your relationship! Simple.

There is solace in being alone. You can think with more clarity when you are alone. Use this time to be your own boss, and make power moves. Stop being so eager to be in a relationship at any cost. If it's not God sent, it's a waste of time. The Bible teaches us to be anxious for **nothing**. Don't feel guilty for leaving a bad situation. You made a decision for yourself to better your life, and that's OK. If you are heart-broken because someone ended a relationship with you, then you need to respect their decision and understand that they were not your chosen mate. It's a relief. Being single is peaceful; Take this time to level up, so you will be ready when your God sent partner arrives.

48. Overthinking

The mind needs time to focus. If you think about too many things at once, you will become confused. One thing at a time! You must not think too much about the same things because you will start to believe your thoughts without proof. If you keep over analyzing every single situation, you risk overriding your gut instincts. Your instincts are powerful, so don't accidently ignore them due to over thinking.

Robert was a wise young man and a great father. He was recently married to Maggie who had the face of a goddess and was stunning from head to toe, the type of beauty that turned heads everywhere she went. Robert was well aware of the attention Maggie received, but it didn't bother him because he was confident in their marriage and sure of himself. One day he sees Maggie's phone light up while she's in the shower. It was her ex boyfriend sending her another text stating that he wants her back and that he loves her. She never responded to the former texts, but when she got out of the shower,

Robert confronted her. She told him that she told her ex to leave her alone, but he keeps texting her. Robert hesitantly believed her, but this incident began to make him feel a little insecure about the attention she attracted. As days passed, he could not get those texts out of his head. He became more and more paranoid, and started imagining different scenarios like wondering if the ex came over while he was at work. He started blaming her and verbally abusing her. Robert was letting the devil attack his marriage during a vulnerable moment. He forgot that God is his protector. Maggie left Robert and went to stay with her parents for a few months. Robert thought he had lost Maggie forever, and had no choice but to seek guidance from the Lord, which led him to becoming a wiser and stronger man.

It turned out that Maggie was telling the truth, and when Robert begged her to come back, she did because she loved him, but she had to show him what he would be missing if he didn't get himself together and also because uncontrolled jealousy can result in dangerous events. Robert almost let his obsessive thoughts ruin his marriage. He knew God showed him favor in this situation, and he definitely learned a good lesson.

49.   Be Compatible

Everyone deserves to be with someone who loves them equally. There are so many people settling, and that's not right. Why settle when you can have it all? You have to stop providing husband and wife benefits for boyfriends and girlfriends. Something else my grandmother would quote is, "Why should he buy the cow when the milk is free?" Stop wasting your time. You're grown, right? Then act like it. You are settling for the wrong men and women. You deserve better. Stop searching and be patient. Exercise discipline in your life. Your king or queen will appear. Two people with two different outlooks on life will always have conflict. You must be willing to wait on the one whom you will become one with just as God and Jesus are one. Having a real connection is something money cannot buy; it's priceless! Having similar hobbies and interests makes the connection stronger because you share the same beliefs and ideals. Having effortless conversations, making each other laugh, and being able to be content with one another during the quiet moments are levels of connections that just don't happen with everyone you are with. That's why you must be patient and let God send you a compatible mate. It's important to be equally yoked. And, it definitely doesn't make any sense for a believer to be with a non-believer. Avoid such people, as they will bring your spirit low.

50. Listen to Her

If your woman is speaking, listen to her. I was born in the eighties but raised by my grandparents who believed in the importance of being a gentleman. Listening means paying attention by listening effectively, and then showing her that you're listening through your actions. So many men hear what their lady is saying, but they are not listening to her. It goes in one ear and right out the other. So pay attention to her. Do not cut her off when she is speaking. Ask questions. Try to really understand what she is saying and how she feels. Show her you were listening through your actions. Miscommunication has ruined too many relationships. Don't take her for granted because there is another man waiting to replace you.

This reminds me of Destiny. She complained to her boyfriend, Melvin, over and over again about needing more quality time with him, but Melvin worked what felt like 20 hours a day because even after he was home, he would continue taking business calls, responding to texts, and replying to emails. Destiny found that although she had spoken to him about this several times, he was making no effort to make even small changes. Even when he was home with her, she felt lonely. So, she spent a lot of time online browsing social media. Eventually she met a younger guy online and he had all the time in the world to talk to her. Messaging turned into texting which soon turned into phone calls. She ended up catching feelings and having an emotional affair with this guy. This was an attack by the devil. The devil roams about seeking whom he may devour. So, his plan is always to attack you when you are in your most vulnerable state. All Destiny needed was for Melvin to listen to what she needed and to make an effort to satisfy those needs for her, but he didn't.

Fellas, be the loyal and attentive man that God made you to be. Cheating is easy. Being faithful in this generation is rare. She needs you to lead her. In order to lead her, you must first carefully listen to her so you can respond correctly. You are the master of your home, so she's watching your response closely. So, don't lose a great woman because you choose to be prideful. Time waits for no one. And ladies, if you're single and/or lonely, remember, God is your first true and real husband. God is real. He's not just some idea in our heads. He is all- powerful and definitely has the power to bless us with contentment when we need it if you continue to trust in Him.

51. Let's Talk: Communication is Everything

Listen! Stop running from one another and talk it out. A couple that prays together stays together. If you don't communicate with your partner and keep them in the dark, they will never know how you feel. How can they attempt to change if you haven't communicated your needs to them? Everyone deserves to be told the truth. It's when you start lying that the lies will continue because one lie leads to the next lie. Keep it 300! Ladies, the main reason men lie to women is because they are scared of how she is going to react to the truth. Try to be approachable and easy to talk to so that your man will feel comfortable coming to you when there is something that is bothering him. Sometimes the truth hurts, but it will always set you free.

52. Relationship Goals

You must work together in order to create a balanced relationship. No one wants to feel like they are in a relationship alone. So many people are married or attached but lonely. How is that possible? Talk to one another. Don't hide things from each other. You need to openly work together to iron out the wrinkles in your relationship. Your partner should be your best friend. Your relationship goals should be to level up spiritually, emotionally, and financially together.

Don't allow any outside forces to interfere with what you guys are trying to build.

53. You too Can Have a Good Man. Yes You!

God has designed a person just for you, but you must be patient in order to receive God's appointed mate for you.

There was a girl named Miracle. She was with a man for 15 years, but they never got married. As the relationship progressed, she began to see his true colors. He was a liar, a cheater, and an abuser, but she stayed with him because they had five children together. She believed him when he would tell her that no man would want her with five kids. She was allowing time invested in the relationship and her children by him to be her reason for staying. Finally, after 15 years of hell, she finally left. She would have never unlocked her blessings had she not leaped out on faith. A few years after she left, she met a deacon at her new church home. This guy made her feel like she could breathe again. He accepted her and her children, and in the first year, they got married, and they have been together for 11 years. See what God did? I can preach all day, but if you don't listen, how can you learn? You have to be fed up with your old life in order to make and see the change you so desperately need! Choices. What the Lord has planned for you cannot be stopped. God's will always happens. Everything happens for a reason.

She thought that no man would ever want her again because of the negative seeds sown into her spirit by her ex. But he was wrong. No man compared to the new man that God brought into her life.

54. Never Cheat

Never cheat because you are unhappy. It will only make things worse. If a person is unfaithful to you, don't cheat to get revenge. Just leave! Never become the person who hurt you. Hit home? You are better than that. Do not cheat yourself out of your blessing. If you cheat, it will make you feel three times worse. Cheating does not bring happiness. Cheating is like a drug. Once you try it, it's addictive. So, you must be under God's protection in order to be safe and resist temptation. Cheating can lead to depression, or even suicide. You never know what someone is going through or how they will react if they find out, so please listen. Don't play with someone's heart. Love is not a game. Love is a powerful word; Use this word with care.

55. One Loyal Woman is Worth More Than 100 Girls

Little boys think they are the man because they have hundreds of girls. I'm the man because hundreds of girls want me but can't get near me. Real authentic women won't submit to a man who is not worthy of leading her. If you are a true king, you will receive honors as such. Trying to keep multiple women happy is trouble. It will tire your mind beyond control. It will break your pockets, deplete your strength, and trouble your spirit. Being faithful to one woman will add to your pockets and add to your wisdom. It's a very simple choice. Loyalty is not only better but for the wise.

And ladies, you have to protect your goodies. Some things are meant for your husband's eyes only. First impressions are everything. Upon first meeting you, your man should know he's dealing with a queen. Lust, desire, and mixed feelings will always be there, but don't let the devil win. It's a test. Don't fail! You must fight with your secret weapon - God's strength and His Word.

56. Respect Women

A woman is indescribably stunning. She carries you for nine months, endures painful deliveries, loves you unconditionally, and raises you. Never disrespect the hand that feeds you with love and honor. Sometimes people can be blinded by the fact that God created women in the image of man. She represents you. So, why not build her up instead of tearing her down? Never hit, belittle, or cheat on your woman. Can you even fathom the thought of a man hitting your mother, sister, or daughter? I didn't think so. This is real talk! Love women for they represent us. Pray for your woman and thank God for her.

57. Keep it 100

Be honest and straight- forward. We're grown, right? No one has time to play games. If you don't genuinely want a person, leave them. Allow them a chance to be with someone who will truly love them. Never hold on to a person just because you don't want to see them with someone else. Do not allow your partner to think that you are more emotionally invested than you actually are. This is very hurtful, and is also an invitation for bad karma to visit you. If you don't love them enough to let go, then do it for yourself! So many people hold on because of their egos, pride, children, or other shared responsibilities. Don't let these things stop you. Break the cycle. It will be hard at first, but be patient; you'll see that you made the correct choice. Always keep it 100 with your mate, and most importantly, always keep it 100 with yourself.

FAMILY, FAITH, AND FELLOWSHIP

58. Protect Your Children

The most precious and most valuable thing in your life is your children. Stop bringing different men around your children. Mothers are devastated everyday to learn that their kids are being molested or abused. If a guy won't respect you, he won't respect your children. The same goes for fathers who bring their children around multiple women then wonder why their sons are so manish. When kids see what their parents are doing, they want to follow the leader because you are their heroes. They look up to everything you do. If you're with a lot of women or men, most likely, your sons and daughters will strive to have a lot of women or men. When you do drugs, it's the same scenario. They'll try it. So you must be a good role model and example before them.

I knew a woman named Reesey. She was 28 and a single mother of an eight-year old daughter when she married her second husband, Nathan, who was 58. Reesey really loved and trusted Nathan. He took good care of her and Nia, her daughter. They did not want for anything which was a relief to Reesey because she really struggled as a single parent. As Nia got older, she began to develop into a beautiful and voluptuous young lady. She would often dance and sing around the house while wearing boy shorts and tight tank tops. Long story short, Nia became pregnant by her step- father at the age of 15, and this is when Reesey also learned that Nathan had been molesting Nia since she was eight years old.

The problem is, you have to be more watchful and not so quick to trust people around your kids. Don't be so thirsty to be with someone. It's okay to be alone and take your time. You must keep in mind that kids are kids and can't think for themselves, so it's our job to protect them and make proper choices for them. For example, when a kid asks to go to a party and they're 13 years old, you might ask the question, "Who's gonna be there?" and they reply, "older kids 18 and 19." You should instantly think *wait a min* (Kevin Heart's voice) *that's not gonna fly*. Anything can happen. It's not safe for a child to party around adults. Like my mother use to say, "Until you turn 18, you belong to me. You don't like it? Tough. I brought you in this world." You know the rest. And to be honest, things can also happen even amongst other kids their own age. So, it's very important to monitor and raise our children with greater wisdom and care.

59. Real Men Take Care of Their Kids

No one should have to tell a man to do for his kids. It takes two to mingle. Right? A lot of people are allowing their new partners to keep their children's mothers and fathers away from their children, but this must stop. It's unacceptable! If the parent is not destructive or dangerous, the children should spend time with their other parent as well.

There was a woman named Yvette. She was the type of woman that was very clingy and spoiled. She liked everything her way. She started dating Steve, a guy that was married with kids, but he and his wife were currently separated. After three months of dating, Steve left the city where his kids and wife lived to move in with Yvette. After living together for a few months, Yvette began to become jealous of the relationship that Steve had with his kids. She felt like he spent too much time visiting them and taking them out, and he wasn't spending enough time with her. She started whining and making him feel guilty because she wanted him to spend more time at home with her.

No real man would allow this to happen under any circumstances. Men, if you have kids by different women, you may regret how you handled things in your past, but they are your kids. So man up or keep your pants zipped up! A good woman should want her boyfriend or husband to take care of his kids. If not, seek marriage counseling or pray for understanding. If she doesn't want to change her way of thinking, she may not be the one for you to marry.

Something else needs to be discussed here also. Men need to take care of their stepchildren too. Fellas, if you marry a woman and she has children, you are marrying those children too. Her kids become your kids and should be treated as such. Yes, often times, the children have an active father, but while the children are at home with you and your wife, they need to be treated with the same love, care, and compassion as your biological children. Too many children are living in blended families and feeling isolated or unwanted. You don't know the damage this type of treatment- even if it's unintentional- is doing to these children. The same goes for women. If you are a stepmother, it is imperative that you treat your stepchildren as if they are your biological children. With so many marriages ending in divorce, it's important that children are exposed to a loving and flourishing family environment.

60. Having Kids Doesn't Make You Mature

This generation's dating behavior has made it difficult for people who truly value being in a loving and committed relationship. With so much baby mama and baby daddy drama and so many side chicks and work boyfriend situations, singles have become weary of the dating scene. In fact, several women have told me that they are not interested in dating men with children because they are tired of dealing with their immaturity and the baby mama drama. Contrary to what many believe, a man who has children can be very mature, and it could be that you were just dealing with little boys posing as grown men. Obviously, some men and women are too young and immature to become parents, so their immaturity combined with the stress of parental responsibilities can result in very drama filled circumstances;

however, sometimes becoming a parent fosters maturity into young men and women.

In order for blended family relationships like these to work, there has to be clear boundaries established between your significant other and their child's mother or father. There has to be respect and understanding amongst everyone involved- the parents and their current partners. Sometimes parents will use their kids to cause trouble and to disrupt their ex partner's new relationship. If you have children by someone other than your current partner, you must set limitations for your ex to ensure that they do not ruin your relationship.

Nowadays it seems that older men with no children are more desirable to women. But, a single, older man can be quite childish. We can all relate to someone like this. Correct me if I'm wrong. Age means experience, and no kids means freedom, so the result is often older men using their wisdom to manipulate younger women who don't understand the game. Maturity has a lot to do with how you were raised and whether or not you have moral standards and not just have them, but live by them. You can be 25 with two kids and ready for marriage or 56 with no kids and still playing childish games. It's 2016 people, so let's grow up and be excellent mothers and fathers to our children! They react to what they see. Let's break the generational curses.

"When I was a child, I used to speak like a child, think like a child, reason like a child; when I became a man, I did away with childish things" (1 Cor 13:11).

61. Love and Respect Your Parents

It states in the Bible that if you do not respect your parents, your days will be numbered (shortened). If you have a spouse that disrespects his or her mother or father, leave now. If they don't respect their parents, they won't respect you. My parents are the best. They instilled the Bible in me at such a young age. My mother is a pastor and an advocate for women, and I miss my dad so much. He taught me a lot of things naturally and spiritually. God rest his soul. I love them so much and strongly believe this is why I have become Mr. King today. I've learned so much because I've made the choice to listen. Nothing but blessings can come to you when you love your parents.

62. Suicide

It's really deep when you begin to have thoughts of hurting yourself. Seek guidance from the Lord, pray that He quiets your heart and eases the pain that you are feeling. If someone is causing you to feel suicidal, you need to remove yourself now before it's too late. My heart is hurting right now because I can't believe that someone would want to take their beautiful life that God created. You have a purpose. Remember that if you take your life, the other person will continue to live on. Put your trust in God and not man because man will fail you every time. People are only human, but God will never forsake you. He will guide you in the right direction.

Focus on yourself instead of contemplating someone who doesn't care whether you live or die. Life goes on and gets better. Just allow yourself the time to heal. I had a friend whose boyfriend would always talk down to her and belittle her. He was constantly telling her that she was not pretty enough or that he wasn't attracted to her. She would become so depressed that she felt like she just wanted to give up on life. I convinced her that the way her boyfriend treated her was merely a reflection of his own insecurities. She eventually built up the confidence to leave him. Don't let people alter your self-esteem. Let them learn from your absence. You're beautiful! Yes you.

63. God is the Only Man You Need at This Time

If it's God's will for you to be married, He will send your assigned mate when he feels you are ready, and when he does, you can trust again. Until then, don't search for a mate because it's on his time; not yours. At one point I wanted everything. I tried everything in the world to get the things I wanted, but failed every time because I wasn't doing it God's way. I was making fast money, taking trips, buying new cars and houses, but nothing ever lasted. Women looked at me as their ideal husband and the answer to their problems not realizing that everything that lasts is through God and not man. You must surrender to God in order to have lasting blessings. Surrender! Don't be hard headed. Be humble and wise. You can do it. I believe in you. Yes you. I went against God's way for years trying to win, but I couldn't. Then, in

2014, my father passed away, and it changed my life. Crippled by my grief, I had nowhere to turn, so I surrendered to God saying, *Have your way Lord. Tell me what you want me to do,* and my life started to take a turn for the better. I started to excel in life. That's when you know you're growing- when doors you never even knew existed start to open.

64. One Day We'll Meet Again

God allows things to happen for a reason. If he reunites a relationship, it is His will, and the couple is now emotionally and spiritually ready for each other. During the break, he was working on you. God never gives you more than you can handle. Sometimes, we lose loved ones, and God uses this time to work on you to ensure that you will see your loved one again in heaven. I know I will see my father again because I will listen to God's instructions to make it in. Sometimes, God takes people away to make you a stronger person. When you love someone more than God, He will remove them from your life. God is a jealous God. Never put anyone before Him. Always remember that experience is the best teacher, and for every setback, there is a greater comeback. Let God work.

65. Be Humble

There's always more to learn in life. Don't ever think that you know everything. Keep your mind open to learning and receiving knowledge so you can make wise decisions. God blesses those who humble themselves. Prideful people always think they know it all, but none know more than our creator. There is always more to learn, but you must humble yourself or your ears will be blocked of knowledge, and we all know that knowledge is power. It's true. It's very important to humble yourself in a relationship so that you understand the issues and make any necessary changes that you need to make. If not, your mate may decide that he or she can always go elsewhere for comfort. This is why most people break up or cheat on one another- lack of humility. Being humble will take you a long way in life.

66. Be a Mentor-Help Others in Need

Everything you go through is for a reason. I promise! Use your experiences to help someone else and support others who are struggling with heartbreak or depression. The world would be a better place if we could learn how to love more, celebrate each other's successes, and be loyal to one another.

I used to know a boy named Kang. As a teenager, he thought he knew everything and

listened to no one. Kang did a lot of regretful things. He was in the streets and mistreating women. He felt like there was no way out of the hell he called life. Countless interventions by family and friends were not enough to bring him back. It wasn't until he hit rock bottom that he surrendered to God and asked for guidance. Would you believe it if I told you that that boy is me? Now look at me. I'm writing a book hoping that I can help to open your eyes and avoid the mistakes that I made because I've been there and done that. Just listen.

67. The Sum of all Fears is Faith

My desire is that I can help as many people as I can in this world to have a better understanding of life, so that they can prepare themselves for growth, not failure. God said that he will make a way of escape for you. My prayer is that this book will be very instrumental to helping many.

When life hits you hard and you don't know what else to do with or for yourself because of a bad relationship or perhaps because your mind and soul desires more, and you fear the outcome of *how, when, what,* and *where,* just stand still and see the salvation of the Lord - the work of his Holy Hand.

The Bible teaches us to wait upon the Lord and he shall renew our strength, and as you are waiting for that assigned mate or waiting to gain the courage to get out of a bad relationship, there are instructions you need to pay attention to:

• Ask God for strength to endure and for the tenacity to say no.

- Occupy your time with creative and innovative people.

- Create your own positive atmosphere.

- Build your mind by reading the bible and other motivational books.

- Tell yourself over and over, "You can do it!"

- Visualize yourself away somewhere really nice, feeling free, and doing something new.

- Do something fun you have never done before.

- Take a trip by yourself and get to know yourself all over again.

- Live, Love, and Laugh.

- Write down your goals and complete them one by one.

Now you are walking in your new, and the *when*, *what*, *where*, and *how* seem to have disappeared. You are on your way because you listened more intensely and found your way. For a new day has arrived.

I want to thank all of my readers for listening and opening up not only your natural ears but your spiritual ears as well.

BONUS CHAPTER

Why Men Cheat

This is for the ladies who are dealing with an unfaithful man. You probably feel like you have done everything right and have gone over and beyond to satisfy your man, yet he still cheats. Well, most women don't understand how men think, so let me try to explain.

Men are a very visual species. When a man sees an attractive woman, he automatically looks at her in a sexual manner. He is checking out her butt, her shape, her hair, her lips, and he is thinking that he would sleep with her if given the opportunity. See, men don't have to know a woman personally or like a woman's personality to want to have sex with her. Although men are visual creatures and thoughts of sex come to mind when they see an attractive woman, men can practice to renew their minds to the point of not always looking at every attractive woman as a piece of meat and a candidate for sex. It's a mindset and the mind can be renewed so that men who desire to become more respectable and honorable men can become just that realizing that sex has its place and is not to be worshipped. Women, however, do not size a man up to determine if he is worthy of sex upon first seeing him. Woman need time to learn about the man and to get to know his personality to determine whether or not he is someone she would sleep with. Men can have sex with a woman without having any emotional ties to her; however, most women won't have sex with a man unless she feels an emotional connection with him. This is why when women cheat it's usually with a guy who's paying attention to her, listening to her, and making her feel special? But when men cheat, it's often with an easy woman with a sexy body. Most men cheat with loose women. Correct me if I'm wrong. I'll wait.

While I'm sure there are countless reasons why men cheat, I'm going to discuss a few of the main reasons.

He is sexually unsatisfied- If a man is not happy with his sex life at home, he will be very tempted to find it elsewhere. This has to do with how often he wants to have sex, what he wants his woman to do in the bed, and what he wants to do to his woman. Men are sexual beings, and in order for him to be happy in the relationship, he must be happy with the sex. This is not to say that a woman should agree to just anything that she is not comfortable doing in the bedroom. Unless a man or woman has a sexually, depraved mindset, he or she won't require anything from his or her mate that's uncomfortable for the mate anyway.

He has lost attraction- Like I said earlier, men are very visual, and they want to feel physically attracted to their woman. They want to like what they see. This doesn't mean you have to be a size two or look like a super-model. This means that you need to be confident because men are attracted to confidence, and you need to take care of yourself and do whatever is necessary to exude your individual beauty. Men are attracted to women who take pride in their appearance, and if a man is not feeling attracted to his woman, he will entertain women who make him feel attracted.

He is bored- Men love excitement and the element of surprise. Sometimes life becomes so mundane, and you'll find that you are having sex on the same days in the same way for the same amount of time. And, although, this may be enjoyable to your husband, he will eventually get bored. Don't be afraid to spice it up every once in awhile. Surprise him with a romantic dinner or new lingerie. As we get older, our sex drive matures. There are levels to this. Channel your inner sexiness to spice up your marriage every now and then.

He is insecure- Believe it or not, insecurity will lead a man to cheating. Sometimes the woman can make her man feel insecure by the way she treats him and speaks to him. And, sometimes a man knows you're too good for him and that you deserve better. He feels insecure about his position in your life and in the relationship, so he will cheat to boost his ego. Getting other women to sleep with him makes him feel good about himself- like he's still got it.

What it all comes down to is value. Does your man value you? And if so, how much? Your man must consider you to be of great value to him. If he feels like he is of more value to you, he will be more likely to cheat. This is also true for women. If a woman considers herself of high value and does not think the same of her man, she will be more likely to arrogant and cheat. Most women will not submit to their man if they doubt his ability to lead her.

So take these life lessons that I've shared with you very seriously. Let it sink in so that you can make the necessary changes that you need to make to attain a better and more blessed life. And remember, a cheater will be a cheater. Cheating happens a lot. But that certainly doesn't mean that you have to deal with it. The choice is always yours.

STAY FREE!!

KING